Walter Pierce

Letters on Insanitary Dwellings and the Housing of the Poor

Walter Pierce

Letters on Insanitary Dwellings and the Housing of the Poor

ISBN/EAN: 9783744792141

Printed in Europe, USA, Canada, Australia, Japan

Cover: Foto ©Suzi / pixelio.de

More available books at **www.hansebooks.com**

THE

LIVERPOOL LAND & HOUSE OWNERS'
ASSOCIATION.

~~~~~~~~~~~~~~~~~~~~~~~~~~~~~

LETTERS ON

INSANITARY DWELLINGS

AND THE

HOUSING OF THE POOR

BY

WALTER PIERCE, PRESIDENT.

OWEN WILLIAMS, TREASURER.

JOHN MURPHY, SECRETARY.

~~~ ~~~~~~~~~

OFFICES, 11, SOUTH JOHN-ST. LIVERPOOL.

———

Reprinted from the 24th Annual
Report of the Association.

———

LIVERPOOL:

WILLIAM SPELMAN, PRINTER, 1 AND 11, SOUTH JOHN STREET.

—

1884.

11, SOUTH JOHN STREET,

LIVERPOOL, 21st *April*, 1884.

SIR,

I am instructed to send you the accompanying Pamphlet, containing a Petition to the House of Commons on "A Bill for the Sanitary Inspection of Dwelling Houses;" also Letters on the important questions of INSANITARY DWELLINGS and the HOUSING OF THE POOR.

I am further to respectfully direct your especial attention to the Tables copied from the Reports of Dr. Taylor, the Medical Officer of Health, which are on pages 33, &c. of this pamphlet, and which show the "Deaths from Fever, Scarlatina, and Diarrhœa in the City of Liverpool during the years 1881 and 1882." The deaths from those diseases are, you will observe, 635 in Front Houses and 329 in Court Houses, showing an excess of the former over the latter of 306.

You will observe the fact that the greatest number of deaths did not occur in houses situate in the narrowest streets. So that from the Tables it is seen that back houses and narrow streets were not in those years at least more insanitary than front houses and wide streets.

It will also be noticed that the deaths from Fever alone in front houses and back houses were, of "Tradesmen 187," "Labourers 173."

It may be inferred, then, that zymotic diseases do not in Liverpool commit their greatest ravages among the lower grade of the working classes, who, it may be supposed, are sparingly fed, badly clothed and uncomfortably housed, among whom indeed great improvidence and wretchedness may, without undue assumption, be said to exist.

In alluding to the above facts I may be allowed to state that they are directly opposed to the theory of those persons who attribute the unhealthy condition of certain portions of the City entirely to the houses, instead of seeking the true cause of it in the habits of a certain class of the community. Such an erroneous theory can tend only to prolong the evil and delay the remedy.

I remain, yours respectfully,

JOHN MURPHY,

SECRETARY.

TO THE HONORABLE THE COMMONS OF THE UNITED KINGDOM OF GREAT BRITAIN AND IRELAND IN PARLIAMENT ASSEMBLED.

THE HUMBLE PETITION OF THE
LIVERPOOL LAND AND HOUSE
OWNERS' ASSOCIATION

SHEWETH,

That your Petitioners are an Association for the promotion of the interests of owners of Land, House, Office, Warehouse, Manufacturing, and other property, from being interfered with by Parliament or other bodies unnecessarily.

That your Petitioners have had under consideration "A Bill for the Sanitary Inspection of Dwelling Houses," which provides for the appointment of Sanitary Inspectors and **that each house and every building in the** United Kingdom shall be visited **at least once every year by a Sanitary Inspector** to make an inspection of the Sanitary fittings, drains, water closets, earth closets, privies, ashpits, cesspools, means of ventilation, water supply and storage, and all other sanitary appliances and things, which means that owners of property and tenants will be put to great expense for plans, inspections and repairs, and that tenants will be subjected to great annoyances by the annual visits, or oftener, of an enormous army of Inspectors that will have to be appointed in addition to those now employed to carry out such a work, thereby creating a very large increase of the present heavy load of Local Taxation, which will lead to considerable additional unnecessary expense to Owners of Property.

It would appear to your Petitioners that the framers of the Bill believe that the bad condition of dwelling-houses

is the principal cause of the high death-rate in the great
centres of population, such as in London, Manchester,
Glasgow,·Birmingham and Liverpool; **this, however,
is not the fact.** But it is a fact that the habits of the
people create the disease. The dwelling houses in the
lower districts have all the new and improved sanitary
arrangements—these being required under the compulsory
powers conferred upon Local Authorities by the provisions
of the Public Health Act, 1875. And, with clean and
thrifty tenants such dwelling houses require no supervision.
The real requirement is, that the dirty and drunken tenants
should be compelled to keep the floors, walls, stairs, and
windows of their houses clean, as well as their own
persons, and punished for neglect; the present custom
being to allow the tenants to accumulate the filth in
houses and to punish the owners of the property as if the
filth was made by them, which is unjust. If decency is
to be enforced, and fever prevented, the contest should be
with the tenants.

The percentage of deaths according to population per
acre in Birmingham is about 47·9, London 50·8, Plymouth
54·0, Manchester 79·8, Glasgow 84·9 and Liverpool 106·3.
In Liverpool the deaths in the two years 1881 and 1882
were from Fever, Scarlatina, and Diarrhœa, in back houses
or courts 329, whilst in houses to the front of comparatively
wide streets the deaths were 635; excess in front houses
306. The back houses for the most part are in narrow
passages or courts, which lead out of very narrow streets,
whilst the front houses, that have the excess of deaths, for
the most part, are in comparatively wide roads, and have
plenty of light and air.

Your Petitioners also point out that there appears to
be an impression, wholly erroneous, that the deaths from
fever are mostly amongst the labouring population, the

fact being that there were in Liverpool 187 deaths from Fever among "the Tradesmen" class in the years 1881 and 1882, whilst the deaths from Fever among "the Labouring" class in the same years were 173, as shown by the Annual Reports of the Medical Officer of Health for Liverpool for the two years referred to.

Your Petitioners humbly suggest that the above figures go to prove that the high death-rate from zymotic diseases is not among the labouring population nor in their dwellings, notwithstanding that they are so very much more numerous than any other class of the population, and where this is found to be the case in Liverpool, the fair inference is that the like results will be found in all other large centres of the population.

It appears to your Petitioners that the effect of the Bill under consideration will be very greatly to add to the present excessive local rates without touching the real causes of the high death-rate, which are in the drunken and profligate habits of the people; besides the greater amount of inspection and " ordering about" proposed by the Bill would harass, day and night, the respectable, clean, well-to-do working men and women, as well as the tenants and occupiers of all the better class of houses in Great Britain, whilst the idle and profligate would escape supervision. A large staff of officials will be an enormous expense to be paid for by the respectable class, who will suffer all the annoyance and inconvenience. And, of course, such an enormous staff would be certain to find out or make plenty of work, as their occupation and existence would depend entirely upon such a result. Houses most certainly are not the causes of disease, and the high death-rate, as may easily be proved on a careful consideration of this question. The law now existing, in the opinion of your Petitioners, is amply adequate for all present requirements as, for example, Section 92 of the Public Health Act enacts :—"It shall be the duty of every "local authority to cause to be made from time to time "inspection of their district with a view to ascertain what "nuisances exist calling for abatement, and to enforce the "provisions of the Act in order to abate the same." Section 96 gives the Justices power to make an order to abate the nuisance and to do any works necessary for that purpose ; and, failing obedience thereto, Section 98 empowers the local authority to do whatever may be necessary, and to recover the expenses incurred by them. Want of food, employment, clothing, and the drunken and profligate habits of the people are the great contributories to the high death-rate of the country and not the state of the dwelling-houses. If the object of the Bill is to reduce the death-rate the real causes should be attacked, and not to wantonly further to diminish the value of property by the employment of an army of Inspectors who are to be paid out of Local Taxation; and, certainly, for no good purpose. And this very great burden will be in addition to the other payments for unnecessary works which owners of property will be subjected to by the Inspectors.

Your Petitioners would point out that it very rarely happens that there are deaths in the same houses or streets in 2 or 3 consecutive years, proving that the houses are not the generators of fever ; if in one year why not in every year. In the opinion of your Petitioners it will be found that there is hardly any greater error than that dwelling-houses generate disease.

Your Petitioners therefore humbly pray
that the Bill do not pass into law.
And your Petitioners will ever pray, &c.
WALTER PIERCE,

LIVERPOOL, 28th April, 1884.   PRESIDENT.

INSANITARY PROPERTY AND THE ISOLATION

QUESTION.

Another crusade is about to set in against the owners of property. A. B. Forwood, Esq. read a paper before the Liverpool Diocesan Conference on the 6th November, 1883, the Lord Bishop of Liverpool being in the chair, in which he suggests that a sum of £1,410,000 should be expended upon removing what he calls insanitary houses.

With all respect to the great intelligence of Mr. Forwood, your Council do not believe that he has yet made out his case—he has not proved that the houses were the cause of the deaths from fever, scarlatina, and diarrhœa, set forth in the tables in the Annual Reports of the Medical Officer of Health for the years 1881 and 1882. Mr. Forwood states that there are 12,000 to 15,000 dwellings that must be dealt with—mainly in 2,300 courts. Now in these courts in the year 1881, only 46 died from *fever*; in front houses 66. From *scarlatina* 32 only died in court houses, and in front houses 108. From *diarrhœa* 28 died in back houses, and 68 in front houses. Excess of deaths in front houses over back houses, 136. Your Council venture to suggest the question—how is it that these diseases are not found in other streets and courts in the City, which are longer, narrower, and in a more filthy condition, if the houses produce the diseases? And how is it that the houses do not produce the like diseases every year? The houses are always the same, but the tenants change and produce the different results by the immoral lives they lead.

In the Medical Officer's Report for 1882, it is stated that there were 1436 cases of fever more than in the previous year. If houses are the sole cause why did they not produce a larger crop during the previous year, because the sizes, shapes, and positions of the houses as well as the lengths and widths of the courts and streets were the same. This year fever was very great in Carlton and Page streets. In the Medical Officer's Report for the previous year these streets are not named, which means that there was not a single case of fever, scarlatina or diarrhœa in either of them. How is this, if property is the producer of these diseases?

In 1882 there were only 137 deaths from *fever* in the 15,000 dwellings in courts. In the front houses there were 237 cases. There were 29 cases of *scarlatina* in back houses and 66 in the front houses. And there were 57 deaths from *diarrhœa* in back houses and 90 in front houses.

But there is another remarkable phase in this question. In the *fever* tables for 1881 and 1882, in Dr. Taylor's Annual Reports, there are 121 streets named; in only 25 out of the whole number did *fever* occur in two consecutive years.

Now the *scarlatina* tables are examined: in 1881 and 1882 there were deaths in 59 streets. In not one of those streets did a death take place in both years. If the houses produced scarlatina in one of the years why not in both?

The *diarrhœa* tables for 1881 and 1882 show that there were deaths in 71 streets, but that deaths took place in only 18 out of the 71 in two consecutive years, showing that there were 53 streets in which deaths from this disease occurred only in one of the same two years.

Surely enough is written to convince any impartial person that houses do not create the three zymotic diseases complained of; the sole cause is in the drunken, dirty, immoral and beastly habits of the inmates of the houses.

In the same house we find a frugal, clean, temperate, healthy person ; he leaves and instead of whom the owner finds he has a low, drunken, dirty, swearing fellow, whose habits breed disease which ends in death. Now, is it fair that the house should be blamed ? The word insanitary should be properly used. Instead of insanitary property it should be insanitary drunkenness, insanitary dirt, insanitary immoral conduct, &c. If the matter be more closely looked into it is easy to show that many of the deaths are in fine, wide, healthy roads, many of which have only very recently, comparatively, been brought into existence, such as Egerton street, Sylvester street, Tatlock street, Wellington road, Boaler street, Robsart street, Chatham street, Brasenose road, Pecksniff street, Rosalind street, &c. Of course Mr. Forwood has no idea of dealing with such streets in his scheme. Or such a street as Beaufort street, which is nearly half a mile long, and 20 yards wide. Deduct all the deaths in such streets and it is astonishing how the insanitary phase of the question is altered. Mr. Forwood should publish the details of his scheme that the public may know as much or more than he understands about it. And we have a right to demand the information since the expenditure of a million and a half of the ratepayers' money is involved in the scheme.

Your President, Mr. O. Williams, your Treasurer, and your Secretary, replied to the misrepresentations made against owners and their property in seven letters, which are given below, as it is considered that all owners of property should be in possession of exact information on this subject, as, in all probability, the City Council might be influenced to interfere greatly with the rights of property. The contents of the letters themselves pretty well explain the subject, so that it is unnecessary to go very much into detail in this introduction and report.

MR. FORWOOD ON INSANITARY PROPERTY AND THE ISOLATION QUESTION.

REPLIES BY MR. WALTER PIERCE, MR. OWEN WILLIAMS, AND MR. JOHN MURPHY.

Reprinted from the "Daily Post" of November 13th, and the "Liverpool Mercury" of November 12th, and December 5th and 20th.

TO THE EDITOR OF THE DAILY POST.

SIR,

I had the privilege of hearing Mr. A. B. Forwood's paper read at the Diocesan Conference, and was present for the purpose of making a few remarks thereon, but the opportunity of speaking was not afforded me, in consequence of the speakers having been already selected. It seemed to me rather unfortunate that none but those prepared to support the views entertained by Mr. Forwood were appointed to speak, as on so important a subject it would have been as well to obtain an expression of opinion from the outside public. I, for instance, entirely disagree with Mr. Forwood's conclusions, and I am inclined to think that the agitation regarding this so-called insanitary property is wholly a mistake, and if permitted to extend will prevent that improvement amongst the lower classes which it is desirable should be encouraged. No one will dispute but that people should live in good habitable houses ; I think there can be little doubt that none but the improvident, the drunken and the dirty do live in uninhabitable houses—made uninhabitable only by the filthy habits of the inmates—whilst others of decent habits in similar houses are in comparative comfort. Drs. Parkes and Sanderson, who were appointed in 1870 to furnish a report on the sanitary condition of Liverpool, state that nothing could exceed the dirt of the people in houses occupied by the improvident and drunken. They report that

the causes of the fœtid atmosphere are the effluvia due to the filth
of the persons and clothes, the effluvia from fish and other food, and
the dirt of the walls, floors, and furniture—where there is any. With
regard to the people and furniture they were not at all prepared
either for the wretched appearance of the people or the terrible aspect
of poverty disclosed. They could not have believed that in any town
in this country they could have gone into room after room, and house
after house, and have found in so many cases literally almost nothing
but the bare walls, a heap of straw covered by dirty rags, and possibly
the remains of a broken chair or table. Many persons had no change
of clothes, and occasionally only washed their hands and face at the
tap. Will Mr. Forwood tell us whether these people would have been
any better off had they occupied a gilded palace under the same
conditions? Messrs. Parkes and Sanderson do not find that there is
insanitary property, but their report attributes the insanitary condition of the town to the insanitary drunkenness and insanitary filth,
and that drink and immorality are the two great causes of the
mortality. They tell us that the causes of this condition of the people
are attributed to the irregularity of the labour market, and the
improvidence, drunkenness, and careless habits of the people. There
is nothing in the report which shows that the owners of property
have been in any way to blame for the unhealthiness of the town.
It appears to me that by attacking property Mr. Forwood begins at
the wrong end, and that the real object we all have, viz., the
amelioration of the condition of the poor, will be ignored and lost
sight of. My remedy would be, first of all, attack drunkenness, filth
and immorality, and when these are conquered, every house in
Liverpool and elsewhere will become a habitable and wholesome
dwelling without the aid of the Corporation or the expenditure of one
penny by the ratepayers.

With regard to the Peabody-buildings, the buildings erected
by Artisans' Dwellings Companies, the Nash-grove buildings, St.
Martin's cottages, and such like schemes referred to by speakers at
the conference, it is well known by Mr. Forwood that the houses are
occupied by a class far above the poor class it is desired to reach, and
that these buildings do not assist in the slightest degree in the
solution of the problem, how to remedy the evils now existing
through drunkenness and its consequent poverty. The Peabody-
buildings, it is acknowledged by the proprietors, have failed in the
purpose the founder intended. Mr. Forwood headed his paper " The

Dwellings of the Industrial Classes." He did not, however, give much information on these, as, indeed, he need not, for it is well known that the buildings now being erected all around Liverpool for the working class are far in excess of the demand. His paper really applied to the very lower class, wherein I have shown he has commenced at the wrong end. I quite admit that for the purpose of beautifying and improving the appearance of the city it is desirable to remove old buildings and to widen narrow streets ; but let it be known that this is what is meant by his paper. He should not mislead the public by the assertion that he contemplates the amelioration of the condition of the poor by building new dwellings. If he stops at merely providing proper shelter he will not help much, and will find his project a failure. He should supplement the benevolence, or to be more efficacious, he should start by providing food and clothing, and assure himself, before transplanting the people to improved surroundings, that they will not speedily reduce the new and improved dwellings to much the same condition as the old abode.

Yours, &c.

WALTER PIERCE.

26, Castle Street, 12th Nov. 1883.

Mr. Walter Pierce's Second Letter.

Mr. Forwood having in a letter made an attack on the Association the following is Mr. Pierce's reply :—

To the Editor of the Daily Post.

Sir,

I see in a letter in to-day's *Post* a remark made by Mr. Forwood to the effect that at the inquiry before Colonel Cox, on the application of the Corporation for a provisional order, "the House Owners' Association, concurring in the views of the distinguished Liberals who opposed the scheme in the Council, were heard." These remarks would imply that the Land and House Owners' Association were taking a political side, whereas the Memorial presented by the Association against the provisional order expressly states that the scheme was unconstitutional and revolutionary, and the memorialists urge that the Liverpool Corporation should be the pioneer in upholding the constitutional law of the realm. In my remarks, also, before

Colonel Cox I stated that the proposed provisional order was one of the most revolutionary and unconstitutional schemes that ever was proposed by a civil body. I do not think that these words would indicate that the Association was taking a political side in the Liberal interests. Mr. Forwood states in his paper read before the Diocesan Conference that, for reasons never explained, the Local Government Board allowed the application for a provisional order to lapse, and in his letter he says :—" In the result the Local Government Board failed to promote the order." The truth is that, in consequence of the opposition by the Land and House Owners' Association and the strong case they made out before the commissioner that the scheme was a confiscation of private property and a deliberate attempt to take property without paying for it, the Local Government Board dismissed the application, and refused to grant a provisional order on the terms applied for.

Yours, &c.

WALTER PIERCE.

26, Castle Street,
Liverpool. 23rd Nov. 1883.

Mr. O. Williams's First Letter.

To the Editors of the Liverpool Mercury.

Gentlemen,

I have read as much of Mr. Forwood's paper which he read at the Diocesan Conference as has appeared in print. Much of it is of little value, as the facts in it about the past of old Liverpool have appeared in print by various writers over and over again. He seems to debit the present owners of property with the condition of our narrow roads and courts, which for the most part, I am informed, were brought into existence about a century ago by the " greed," as he calls it, of our merchant princes ; certainly before " a Welsh jerrybuilder " was ever known. Those narrow streets and courts were brought into existence by the then demands of the commercial class, when wages were very low indeed ; the lower the wages the smaller the house and the narrower the streets and courts—this seems to have been their theory. And the great feature of this paper is to provide dwellings at the expense, mainly, of owners of property, for the lowest class of poor who load and unload ships. Surely the merchants should provide houses for this class, so that they may reside in mercantile model cottages. Such houses, no doubt, would pay them well, according to their notions of the cost of such houses. For all the other classes there is an ample supply of dwellings, especially for the working classes. I cannot find that our merchant princes—those who make the most noise about insanitary property—uplift as much as their little finger to provide better houses for the working classes than those in existence. No better houses can be found in the kingdom, both in plan and construction, than the four and six roomed houses now being built in Liverpool. They are much better than any five-deckers. Those which were built by the Corporation were intended as a pattern to builders, to show them that better houses could be erected for the working classes, and to pay builders for doing so better than the ordinary houses. And with what result? The dividends or interests show only about 3 per cent. Would any of the advocates for five-deckers build houses on their own account and be satisfied with 3 per cent., for the frugal class, such as are to be now found in the Sylvester street four and five-deckers, or that will inhabit the Nash-grove houses? I mean the frugal class, not the improvident. Could our builders afford to build and live on such results? Merchants and shipowners should stick to matters they understand better than housebuilding. But if they feel more for the condition of the working man than present builders do why do they not turn to and build better houses out of their own means, and not out of the corporate funds, which means increased local taxation, and which, again, is contributed for the most part by owners of property and not by the merchant class? If this class do feel more than any other let them agree to advocate for or to promote a bill to contribute towards local taxation exactly as they do towards national taxation. Let them contribute out of their net profits pound for pound with owners of property. No; the burden of Mr. Forwood's paper is that the great changes—the great transformation of old Liverpool into a new Liverpool —shall take place, but not at the expense of personalty, but at that of property, which for local taxation contributes about six times as much as personalty. Why not do away with the principle of the poor-rate assessment, and collect local taxation on the same schedules as national taxation? Then a rate of 1s. in the pound would yield as much as 6s. does under the present poor-rate assessments. Let all profit contribute alike, and it will be very easy to change old Liverpool into a comparatively rural district, with its playgrounds, squares, boulevards, and parks; and the burden would be light to all tax-payers out of net profits.

Another fallacy which runs through Mr. Forwood's paper is that the decrease of the death-rate is due to what he calls sanitary science. It is a fact that the people are very much better fed now than formerly. Has this feature had anything to do in reducing the death-rate? In 1840 the consumption of sugar was about 15 pounds per head of the population, now it is about 59 pounds. Of corn, wheat, and wheat flour, the consumption in 1840 was 42·47 per head, whilst in 1878 it was 188·29. Of tea: In 1840 the consumption per head was 1·22, in 1878 it was 4·66. Rice: In 1840 the consumption was 0·90, whilst in 1878 it was 7·50. Potatoes: In 1840 it was 0·01, whilst in 1878 it was 28·96. Eggs: In 1840 the consumption was 3·63, in 1878 it was 23·18. Bacon and Ham: The consumption in 1840 was 0·1, whilst in 1878 it was 12·60. And so on for other articles, such as butter, cheese, currants, raisins, &c. These factors are conveniently left out of calculation when credit is being taken for *sanitary science* having reduced fever and the death-rate.

Drunkenness has decreased very greatly. Has this anything to do with reducing the death-rate? In 1875, 21,694 cases were before our magistrates; in 1882, the number was 16,003. In 1875, the population was 516,063; in 1882, it was 560,377.

A large number of the most ignorant, improvident, and wretched fall into the grave yearly, and a much better educated class appear on the stage to take their place. Has this feature had anything to do with reducing the death-rate?

Of all the prisoners who appeared before the justices last year for offences, only 2·5 per cent. could read and write well, and of drunkards only 3·1 per cent. An improved education of the working class is bound to make itself felt on the death-rate; and the improved education even of those who now appear before the justices is already very perceptible.

It may not be uninteresting to Mr. Forwood, the general public, and our medical men throughout the country, to know in what proportion the very lowest of our population in Liverpool contribute towards the general death-rate of the city by fever, scarlatina, and diarrhœa, as disclosed by the annual reports of the Medical Officer of health for the

B

city and port for the years 1881 and 1882, as likely similar causes will have produced similar results in most thickly-populated districts in other large cities and towns. In the annual report for the year 1881, page 5, are the words—" The extensive sanitary operations carried out during the last 20 years have greatly diminished the prevalence of fever." Is this so? Another statement is the following :—" Every local outbreak is the result of poverty, dirt, and improvidence," And " very few cases can be attributed to poverty alone " is another statement in this report. " The tenant of the house earned plenty of money and spent it in drink " is a fourth statement. " The people were intemperate and the houses in a filthy condition " is a fifth statement. " The house was very dirty " is another. Now, from the foregoing, the general impression of the public, no doubt, is that most deaths from fever, scarlatina, and diarrhœa would be amongst the very lowest of the population and in the narrowest streets and courts, in which the sun can hardly ever reach the pavement the year round, by reason of the streets and courts being so very narrow, and, of course, courts are even much narrower than are the streets out of which they lead. In page 21 of the report for 1881 is a table giving a list of the streets in which there were two or more deaths from fever. In front houses there were 66, in back houses 46. On page 25 is a table showing the list of the streets in the city wherein three or more deaths from scarlatina occurred. In front houses 108, in back houses 32. On page 28 is a table showing three or more deaths in streets in the city during the year from diarrhœa. In front houses 68, in back houses 28. Total deaths in front houses from fever, scarlatina, and diarrhœa, 242 ; in back houses, 106 ; excess of deaths in front houses over back houses, 136. On page 23 of the same report is a table giving the occupations of persons who had died from fever in their houses in the city, excluding deaths in workhouses and hospitals in 1881. Labourers 66, tradesmen 72, excess of tradesmen over labourers 6, which is a curious fact. But in the parish workhouse and hospitals there were 51 labourers against 31 tradesmen. In West Derby Union Workhouse, labourers 6, tradesmen 8. In Everton Hospital, Netherfield road, labourers none, tradesmen 4 ; giving a total result of only 8 more labourers than tradesmen, which is another curious fact to be studied, because the general impression is, no doubt, that the deaths are very much more numerous among the very poorest, the dirtiest, most improvident, and drunken of our population than among the trades-men class of the city. On page 8 of the report it is stated that " the patient should be isolated, and all communication with neighbours and visitors cut off." Of course this should be so. But does it not, in effect, take place already, as the great death-rate appears among the tradesmen class, not among the very lowest of our population. Surely, in the homes of the tradesmen class there are extra rooms in which patients can be isolated; I mean kept pretty well apart from the other inmates. If so, surely this is isolation as much so as in a hospital. If this be admitted, we have only to deal with fever cases, &c., among the labouring class. On looking closely at this isolation doctrine, it does not appear that fever and the other zymotic diseases spread very rapidly, when not more than two or three cases are found in streets over 100 yards along. And these two or three cases are a long way apart from each other. Rarely are two cases found in the same house, showing that fever does not spread like leaven, attacking those in the same house or the residents of the adjoining houses. In effect, is this isolation? This is written with the object of inviting a closer study of the question, for it is very easy to create alarm on such a question as this, when there should be none. The idea seems to be to erect large and expensive buildings in which to isolate patients, which means another great increase of local taxation. Dr. Taylor should be asked to give the number, width, and length of narrow streets, and the number of front and back houses, in which there was not a single case of fever, scarlatina, and diarrhœa during the last or the previous year, and the like with reference to those in which those diseases existed. The public should be supplied with the information necessary to enable them to see all around this question. It will soon be seen that houses do not generate the diseases, because the very worst houses and the very worst streets were quite free from the diseases. And if houses do not generate the principal diseases complained of, it should be found out what is the real cause. If discovered, the cause should be dealt with in some practical and determined manner, instead of wasting money on those cases which do not generate disease. One remedy would be to serve all sanitary notices on tenants in the first instance, so as to give owners and agents more power to deal with the most improvident tenants. If decent the owners would be certain to deal with the sanitary notices when presented to them by tenants. If not, the tenants should be punished and ejected from the houses. The lowest class of tenants are much worse and dirtier than 40 years ago, when owners had more control. Now if an owner uses any pressure for rent or on account

n 2

of drunkenness or other cause the house is dirtied as a punishment
of the landlord by the tenant. My suggestion might be tried for a
year or two. And all distress warrants should be executed by the
police or County Court bailiffs, owners paying the cost. In this way,
tenants would soon be made to feel that the house would have to be
kept clean and the rent paid or they would be ejected therefrom. In
this way property would not be wrecked, and there would be a great
control over the lowest tenants, and no riot or disturbance. When a
warrant is executed by the police or County Court there are no
disturbances as a rule.

In 1882 there were 1486 cases of fever more than in 1881. In this
year's report, page 6, are the words—" Fever is generally associated
with insanitary property and crowded courts and alleys." Is this so ?
What do the above figures disclose ? Do tradesmen reside in courts
and alleys or in front houses? The greatest death-rate was in front
houses and among the tradesmen class—not labourers. Fever seems
to have made great havoc in Page street and Carlton street in the
year 1882; but in the Medical Officer's report for the previous year
no case of fever is mentioned in either of those streets. If streets
and insanitary property are the cause how is it that we do not find
cases of fever and other insanitary diseases in the same courts, alleys,
and houses year after year ? The truth is that there were thousands
of small houses in the narrowest streets and courts free from those
diseases. But can the cause be fairly traced to the houses as such in
which the poor and tradesmen class died? The two reports referred
to trace the cause of the high death-rate to other causes, not the
state of the houses. The houses are the same every year, but the
people and their habits change; it is this that brings about the different
results. Money is to be lavished on improved dwellings as if the
dwellings caused all the filth, drunkenness, improvidence, &c. complained of by Dr. Taylor in the reports. The sober, frugal, and
industrious class get along very comfortably in the present dwellings.
Good dwellings exist for such. And what is the City Council about
to do ? They are about to try to provide as good or better dwellings
for such ; but what is to be done for the improvident, the filthy, the
drunkards ? Such will not be admitted into the Nash Grove houses.
Out of them the high death-rate comes. Those tenants who are
admitted into the Sylvester street four and five-deckers, and who
will be admitted into the Nash Grove houses, have very good
characters already. How will the houses, the bricks and mortar,

improve them? They are to be left in their present houses, I suppose. No landlord will have them in good houses. How, therefore, will the death-rate be improved? Five-deckers are to be erected on the Nash Grove site, and a keeper and collector will be employed, to reside on the spot, to take care that only decent, respectable working men will be allowed to enter any of these dwellings. Again, I have to ask, how is the death-rate to be lowered if the poor and wretched portion of the population are to be compelled to reside in their present abodes, as argued by Mr. Forwood? The City Council are about to waste a very large sum of money in the erection of the Nash Grove houses. And for what? The ratepayers will not derive anything from the large expenditure, because there are at present plenty of better houses for the class that will be admitted into those houses. I mean the sober and frugal class, not the dirty drunkards. Reference is made to the Peabody and other houses in London. Why, it is admitted that the occupiers of those houses are of a much higher class than that which it is now proposed to erect the five-deckers for. And Mr. Forwood must know this, because it has been disclosed in evidence. In my opinion it is a very great mistake to crowd such a number of people on an acre of ground. Fancy some thousands of the lowest of our population being brought so near to each other, and fancy a row breaking out. What chance would the police have? Hitherto they have been comparatively successful, because the population are so spread. The poorest should be spread over the largest area possible, both for health and for police purposes.

In 1882 there were 237 cases of fever in front houses and 137 in back houses. There were, in 1882, as many as 66 scarlatina cases in front houses and 29 in back houses. In 1882 there were 90 cases of diarrhœa in front houses and 57 in back houses. Died of above in front houses, where the air was pure and plentiful comparatively, 393 cases—in back houses 223—showing more in front than in back houses 170 cases, notwithstanding that the court houses are most numerous in the fever, &c. streets. So much for Mr. Forwood's song against narrow, dark, dingy back houses! From this point of view are wide roads and plenty of light and air in favour of a low death-rate? I believe they are; but not for the reasons given by Mr. Forwood. The number of labourers who died at home of the above diseases was 107, of tradesmen 115. I am sorry to notice the feeling evinced against owners of property. Old and new houses are erected for the convenience of the commercial class. Owners of small houses—old or

new—are too often looked down upon and treated as if they were
criminals. From the treatment builders often meet with from the
authorities it might be a crime to build new houses; as if they
should give up their property for the benefit of the public without
payment. Do the commercial class give up their ships and other
property without payment? Owners, as a rule, never expect to be
paid more than the value of the property when taken from them.

Yours truly,

32, Castle street.   O. WILLIAMS.

Mr. O. Williams's Second Letter.

To the Editors of the Liverpool Mercury.

Gentlemen,

On the 12th instant you were so good as to allow a long letter from
my pen to appear.   There was a general impression that the death-
rate from fever, scarlatina, and diarrhœa was very much greater in
back houses than in front houses.   In that letter I pointed out that,
according to the tables published in the Medical Officer's reports for
1881 and 1882, there were 306 deaths more in front houses than in the
2300 back houses.   Also, that 187 tradesmen died of those diseases, as
against 173 labourers, notwithstanding that the number of the latter
is greatly in excess of the former.

I have now to direct the reader's attention to another phase of the
question, to endeavour to prove that houses do not generate those
diseases which are attempted to be fastened upon property by Mr.
Forwood.   In the years 1881 and 1882 there are 121 streets named
in Dr Taylor's annual reports in which there were deaths from *fever*.
But only in 25 of those 121 streets did fever occur during the two
consecutive years.   The roads were the same widths and lengths, and
the houses and courts the same,   If they generated fever in 1882 why
not in 1881, and if in the latter why not in the former years?   Now
we deal with the *scarlatina* tables in the same way.   There are 59
streets named in the two annual reports.   In not one of the 59 streets
did a death take place from scarlatina in the same street in each of
the two years.   Again, if the streets, courts, or houses generated
scarlatina one year why not in both?   The *diarrhœa* tables for the
two years show that there were deaths in 71 streets ; also, that deaths
took place only in 18 out of the 71 streets in both years.   Surely, this

is proof sufficient that houses are not the cause of death, but that it should be traced to something else. The sole cause is in the drunken, dirty, immoral, and beastly habits of the tenants.

Mr. Forwood talks a good deal about raising the condition and habits of the people by placing them in good houses. Four or five-deckers are in the possession of the Corporation situated in Sylvester street. Those 146 houses at present are tenanted by sober, industrious, frugal persons, who behave themselves and pay their rents. Of what value are those tenements to the low dirty fellows who breed fevers, scarlatina, diarrhœa, and other zymotic diseases, so long as they are kept outside of them? I and others have the opportunity of looking at the outsides of them, and so have the drunkards. By way of experiment how would it do to turn all the tenants out of the Sylvester street four and five-deckers and to put the drunkards and the vagabonds in them instead by way of improving their condition and reducing the death-rate? Being improved, of course, the result would be all right at the end of the year, and their rents all paid up! Now, reader, do not smile; I am serious, for it would be very much more reasonable to make this experiment than to spend a million and a half of money, and then to have found out that houses, after all, would not improve the morals of the people. It is not a house, or bricks and mortar, or paint and paper, that will raise the condition of an individual. Man is free to reduce himself lower than the level of the beast; also, he is free under gracious influences so to improve and elevate himself as that he might become a benefactor to the whole human race. Put a man lost to self-respect in a marble palace and he will soon show you that it is little better than a marble stye of filth.

An experiment was tried. The Corporation purchased a large plot of land in Sylvester street, with the intention of covering the whole of it with four and five-deckers, I suppose. But a portion only was covered, and the remainder of the land was sold at a very great loss to the ratepayers. Another experiment is being tried in Nash grove, which is wrong in principle. The intention is to let houses at less than their natural rentals. If a tenant cannot pay the proper natural rent of the day he should go to the Select Vestry or the Board of Guardians. It is their duty to deal with such matters. The Corporation are, to my mind, going beyond their province in dealing out charity to the poor. If a man must have a shilling loaf and has only ninepence to pay for it he goes to the Select Vestry for assistance.

The matter of rent should be similarly dealt with. But there is another feature of the question that should be considered. Are court houses unhealthy ? What is it that makes them so ? Are the rooms too small ? Is there no other way of dealing with them than to pull them down ? The house parts, of course, are all right, as the doors, are invariably open during the day. Can more air be let into the bedrooms without creating draughts ? Can the rooms be ventilated ? Let the Sanitary Committee employ Mr. Joseph Leather to ventilate some of the very worst bedrooms in the city, as an experiment. The air about Sylvester street is very bad. It is difficult to find worse. If tenants can live and be tolerably healthy there, they can live so anywhere in the city. I have no manner of doubt that Mr. Leather can give the tenants as good air in the insides of the houses as that on the outside. Should he do so, then there will be no occasion to pull houses down on account of want of sufficient air.

Before leaving the death-rate question, I should mention that very many deaths have taken place in fine wide roads, in some without a single court house, and in others with only a very few courts. Of course, Mr. Forwood does not intend to do anything to those streets of houses. If the deaths be deducted in these streets, it is astonishing how altered is the whole death-rate question. Mr. Hawksley, in Liverpool, when president of the Social Science Congress, stated that Sanitary Science has not contributed one atom towards the reduction of the death-rate, notwithstanding that hundreds of millions have been expended directly and indirectly in the attempt. I suppose this gentleman will be admitted to be as great an authority as Mr. Forwood on this question, for no living engineer has had more to do with such works than he has. We should therefore be very careful before embarking in a scheme that will entail an expenditure of £1,410,000 as estimated by Mr. Forwood.

Well, now, just for the sake of the argument, I will suppose that this large sum is to be expended. By whom ? By one section, or by the whole community ? Is Mr. Forwood prepared to pay his share ? Is he personally prepared to pay pound for pound with property ? Is it not fair that all net profit should contribute alike towards such a Christian object, whether the profit be from property or the net profit from personalty ? Mr. Forwood, of course, must be prepared to do his share, as the thing is so reasonable, and because he sets himself up as a preacher, a pattern, and an example to all others. Read the following from his paper read before the Diocesan Conference. Of course, the tone is rather higher and lofty, which the reader might be prepared to expect, as it was to be delivered in the presence of the Lord Bishop, a large gathering of "the cloth," and the cream of the laity :—" Above all Christianity will benefit, as the people will see that its doctrines are not idle, hollow precepts, without life, but that they influence men to practice that which they preach." Yes, of course, Mr. Forwood will, after this, practice that which he has preached. When the Master was on earth He was the pattern, because He was very much above all and practiced that which He preached. Also, He was a real example only to those who believed in Him and were prepared to make sacrifices to follow His teaching. But His holy life and lofty precepts only created guilt, condemnation, and spiritual death in those who only preached, pretended, and did not perform. Yes, people believed in the Master because He was above all others. Mr. Forwood pretends to be above us all, or to be the leader in this matter. Surely he is willing to pay pound for pound, according to his income, with a poor " Welsh jerry-builder," to bring about such a change. This is a very low level to place the question upon, namely, to be on a level with owners of small cottages and poor builders. " Do not even the publicans the same ? " But Mr. Forwood is on a high pedestal ; and because he has chosen this elevation we expect from him as much as that which every owner of property will have to contribute ; and what is that ? Mr. Forwood states that the sum of £14,538 is a little more than the yield of a rate of one penny in the pound on the poor rate assessment over the whole City. I will then assume that a penny rate will yield within this area say about £14,000. Under the Income and Property Tax schedules, for national taxation, within the same area a penny will yield about six times as much, or £84,000. Owners of property have to pay on their net profits towards Local as well as National Taxation. Mr. Forwood does not. Our contention is, that he and all personalty should ; that all net profit should pay alike both for National and Local Taxation. Let this be brought about and such a scheme would be light on all ; if it has to be borne by only one section—property—the tax will be a great addition to the present heavy load of Local Taxation. £84,000 as the yield of a penny rate on the Income and Property Tax schedules would pay interest on a loan of say £2,500,000, whilst £14,000, the yield of a penny rate under the Poor Rate assessment, would only pay interest on say £400,000. Had we Local Taxation resting on the Income and

Property Tax schedules the ratepayers would soon feel the great power in a penny rate. Our city might be improved and ornamented, and old Liverpool might be changed into a semi-rural city in a very short time, without any burden upon any. Until Local Taxation is made to rest upon a proper principle it is impossible that changes on a large scale can be made upon the houses or streets.

And now is the very time to agitate for such a change—to bring personalty under contribution. Our municipal body passed a resolution, after hearing evidence, affirming that personalty should be brought under contribution; but the municipality has stopped with the passing of the resolution. It is now well known that the Government are about to introduce a bill to alter our present system of Local Taxation. A deputation to Mr. Gladstone to urge the question, and to submit to him the resolution passed by the City Council might have a very good effect. And Mr. Christopher Bushell, who moved the following resolution at the Diocesan Conference, should most certainly join such a deputation, as his venerable appearance and the eloquence he usually brings to bear upon all works of Christian charity would do great good. But his preaching also should end in practice. The following is the resolution which was carried by the meeting:— Mr. Christopher Bushell, who followed, proposed—"That this conference, feeling deeply that a provision of healthful dwellings for the working classes is, in the interest of the spiritual and moral welfare of the community, a subject of first and highest importance, desires to urge upon the City Council of Liverpool that they do put in force as speedily as possible the powers which they possess for the acquisition, and, where needful, for the demolition of insanitary dwellings, and that careful regard at the same time be had to the absolute need for due provision of suitable dwelling accommodation for those who may thereby be dispossessed. Further, this conference desires to impress upon the urban sanitary authorities in the diocese, the earnest fulfilment of their duty to take immediate steps for the improvement, and, if needful, the demolition, of insanitary dwellings in their respective districts."

In my humble opinion, Mr. Forwood has not yet made out a case, that houses do generate the diseases which go greatly to increase the death-rate in Liverpool; therefore, I do hope the Council will not expend £1,410,000 for such an object. More than the first half of his paper is written in very bad taste, treating of matters many of which were disposed of in Dr. Duncan's and Dr. Trench's days. But he is fond of exaggeration and hard words if he thinks they will serve his then object. I do not envy his talent. He finds fault with the avarice of owners and builders in not making better sewers. What had either, as such, to do with them? His own class, personalty, were in power then as now at the head of affairs. It was their fault, not that of the builders. He seems in his paper to have scraped together every scrap of history which he thought might influence the ignorant against the owners of small property. A more frugal, honest, industrious class does not exist in Liverpool. By their frugal habits they save until they have got together a small capital, which some of them invest in the building of small houses, whilst others invest their little savings in building societies. And this, as a class, is that which are the owners of nearly all the small property. And this is the class that Mr. Forwood seems to think so lightly of and of their hard earnings and property. The capital of the mortgagee, of course, must be protected, but there seems to be no sympathy whatever for that of the mortgagor. It is the poor mortgagor that is first hit by these changes and by the increase of Local Taxation. In 1847 the rates were about 2s. 6d. in the pound; now they are about 6s. 8d. in some districts. And this is the class that will have to bear Mr. Forwood's large expenditure unless personalty will contribute. He tells us that there were only a few windows in the days of the window tax. What had that to do with the present question? Why did not the wealthy of the day build better houses and construct wider roads in 1840. The rich class did no more in the way of putting the labouring man in good houses out of their own means then than they are now doing. I conclude this letter by stating that the most of the charges that go to make up Mr. Forwood's poor miserable paper against owners and builders of property really do not belong to them, but should be laid at the doors of those gentlemen in authority and of those who were best educated of the day and had the largest amount of capital. They neglected their duty; hence the present state of the question.

In my opinion, every court house, all narrow streets—indeed, nearly all old Liverpool—should pass into history, which might easily be done if personalty were brought into contribution for that purpose. It is of no use to go on patching and tinkering, as in the past, which has been little better than a waste of money. In the meantime, I recommend that all sanitary notices in the first instance should be served upon owners. Warrants of distress and ejectments should be executed by legal officers—the police. Lodging-house sleeping rooms should be ventilated at the public expense by way of experiment, and a jet of light should be put into each trough closet.

Yours truly,

O. WILLIAMS.

32, Castle Street, 23rd Nov., 1883.

Mr. O. Williams's Third Letter.

TO THE EDITORS OF THE LIVERPOOL MERCURY.

GENTLEMEN,

I did expect a little better treatment at the hands of Mr. Campbell; from him I expected "a cup of cold water" for having discovered that the greatest death-rate from fever, scarlatina, and diarrhœa, is not in the alleys, courts, or hovels, but in front houses.

2. That scarlatina did not repeat itself in any one of the streets named in Dr. Taylor's tables for the years 1881 and 1882.

3. That fever and diarrhœa repeated themselves in a very few instances comparatively during the same two years.

4. That the greatest death-rate from fever, scarlatina, and diarrhœa is not among labourers, but among tradesmen. These facts are very curious, and suggest new lines of thought. If the £200,000 be borrowed, will it be applied in pulling down the houses in which the greatest death-rate exists?

5. Mr. Campbell states that the tenants pay the taxes—not the owners—because they are the great consumers. Well, let us see where this view will lead us to. Suppose we admit, just for the argument, that this is so. At present the Local Taxation in West Derby is about 6s. 8d. in the pound, in 1847 it was 2s. 11d. In Everton, in the same year, the Local Taxation was 2s. 2½d. in the pound; in 1882 it was about 6s. 8d. Is it right and just that the great working class should pay this high rate? If personalty be brought into contribution a rate of 1s. in the pound will bring in as much as the present total income. Of course the working man would be much benefited if he had to pay only one-sixth for Local Taxation that which he now pays. But would that be just? This is one side of the question.

6. But there is another. A farm (all the other things being equal) tithe-rent free sells for more money than one subject to tithes ; and property subject to light taxation sells for more money than when subject to high taxation. Taxation in some of the out-townships has increased fully one-third since 1847, and property has decreased in value in the same ratio.

7. I believe it would be just to bring personalty into contribution, so as to give our representatives ample power to improve and beautify our city, as well as to improve the social condition of sections of the people.

8. One shilling in the pound would bring in about as much money as the present rates do.

9. Twopence in the pound more would enable all old Liverpool to be transformed into a semi-rural city.

10. Another penny in the pound, or £84,000 per annum, would enable Samuel Smith, Esq., M.P., to deal with his question of the children of widows—to feed, clothe, and educate them up to a point, so as to fit them for emigration or otherwise, so that their mothers would be free to go into service or into other employments. Until we shall have dealt with the condition of the children of widows we shall always have the shocking sights in our streets that are now so common. It is impossible that a widow by her own labour can earn sufficient to feed, clothe, pay rent, and educate her children. It is therefore the ratepayers' duty to do so.

11. Another penny in the pound would yield another £84,000 per annum. With such a sum, the public-house question might be handled. Compensation might be paid out of it to owners and occupiers.

12. I am charged with being selfish. My income is from personalty, very little from property. Mr. Patterson has his income from the disposal of wheat, flour, &c.; mine from the sale of land and property—both of us from personalty. I am willing that personalty shall be taxed—though it will take more out of my pocket yearly—if Mr. Patterson is, because I consider the principle just. I am not willing to sit down in the midst of all this wretchedness with my arms folded without making an effort to bring about some improvement. Mr. Patterson, no doubt, is very able both in the use of his pen and tongue. I wish I could get him to see with me that an altered system of Local Taxation would give our City Councillors an immense power to wield for good.

Unquestionably commerce is a very great agent in adding to the wealth, comfort, and happiness of all classes in this country—merchants, owners, and the working class—and all should contribute alike towards National and Local Taxation out of their net profits.

Mr. O. Williams's Fourth Letter.

To THE EDITORS OF THE LIVERPOOL MERCURY.

GENTLEMEN,

With the first dip of ink I wish to acknowledge Mr. Campbell's expressions of kindliness towards myself. In every word I may write on the very important questions under consideration I hope to reciprocate it.

I am glad to find that the views of Mr. Campbell and my own on several questions already discussed are much the same. He is most anxious that all court houses and narrow streets should pass into history; so am I. But I appear to wish the transformation to be made in a shorter time than he does, and that personalty should assist. I am anxious that all old Liverpool, or nearly so, should be pulled down and the land laid out again according to modern sanitary notions, very much in the same way that Paris was dealt with by the late Emperor. I saw old Paris, threaded many of the narrow roads, and was shocked by the sight of the miserable tumble-down structures. A few years afterwards I visited Paris again, and was astonished at the change that had been made. The transformation appeared as if it had been brought about by the touch of the wand of the harlequin. Well, such a change in so short a time would have been impossible on our system of Local Taxation. Their system of Local Taxation is very similar to that of their National Taxation, though the former is a little more mixed. The burden of my song has been for many years to bring about a scheme, based on justice, which would give our administrators more money, and therefore more power to bring about great changes in a comparatively short time.

Mr. Campbell does not seem satisfied with our present system of National Taxation; nor am I with the feature of the indirect Taxation, such as taxing tea, coffee, cocoa, tobacco, &c. In my opinion, the principle on which the Income and Property Tax schedules rest—of course, I speak generally—is sound. Personalty or trade pays on the net profit, and so does property. Where there is no profit there is nothing to pay. On this principle I do not see how commerce is interfered with. If a merchant has made a net profit of £1000, and if a rate of 1s. in the pound is made, of course £50 is taken from him. In like manner if an owner of property has made a net profit of £1000, he also has to contribute £50 towards Imperial Taxation. This is the present principle and practice in our direct portion of our system of National Taxation ; and I do not hear any complaints about the principle. The complaints are about the mode of assessments and collections. There need be no difficulties if parties will make faithful returns. This is the principle, because it is just, which I wish applied to Local Taxation. I will wait for Mr Campbell's views on this feature before I give my reasons for applying the same principle to Local Taxation. If I can obtain his consent to the former, I fancy we shall not be very far apart from each other when our views are known to each other on Local Taxation.

I thought I had travelled with Mr. Campbell when I admitted, for the argument, that the consumers do pay all Taxation—National and Local—when paying owners are only as agents for tenants. Having done so, in effect I asked which was the friend of the working man—Mr. Campbell, who requires him to pay 6s. 8d. in the pound, or Mr. O. Williams, who by the proposed system would only take 1s. in the pound from him? Mr. Campbell asks me if it is not quite time that a squaring should take place between land and property owners ? What is meant by this sentence ? The great political economist Mr. Macqueen has written that the building of property is as much a business as the building of ships or of any branch of commerce, and is liable to similar fluctuations of profit and loss. I will answer every question Mr. Campbell may put to me as far as I can, and shirk nothing.

With respect to the question of there being more front than back houses in the streets in which the diseases of fever scarlatina, and diarrhœa were, of course I know nothing more than is found in Dr. Taylor's tables. I have simply dealt with the streets in the tables. In some streets named I know there are very many more back than front houses. For instance, in Mann-street there is a house on the corner of each side of a court, whilst there are ten or twelve houses behind in the court. And Mann-street is very long. I mentioned in my letters that much more information was required from Dr. Taylor before exact conclusions could be drawn. We should have the percentages of front as against back houses in the streets in which the diseases existed. Indeed, I applied to Dr. Taylor for information which would have made the figures I published more complete. On finding that the trouble and loss of time would have been great to the Health Department to obtain, I abandoned the idea.

Until we agree about our present system of levying taxation under the Income and Property Tax Schedules, it will be of no use discussing the justice of applying the principle for the purposes of Local Taxation

As Mr. Campbell makes frequent references to political questions in his letters, with a view of shortening and narrowing the issue between us it is quite as well that he should understand something about my political creed. I am a disciple and a very humble follower of Mr. Cobden and Mr. John

Bright. As one of the council of the Financial Reform Association I
assisted to obtain the present measure of free trade, and I neglect no opportunity to assist to obtain another instalment.

As far back as the year 1869 I wrote eleven letters, which appeared in
your paper, advocating direct taxation and the repeal of the Customs and
Excise duties. Afterwards they were published in the pamphlet form. Soon
afterwards the scheme of doing away with custom houses was considered at
two rather large representative meetings in the office of the late Mr. Robertson
Gladstone, at which I was present. Of course, the licensing question was
the chief difficulty then as now. Mr. Bright did not commit himself to the
scheme. but he evidently thought favourably of it. His views, if my
memory is correct, were pretty fully expressed at a meeting in the
Philharmonic Hall soon afterwards. I had the honour also of meeting Mr.
Cobden soon afterwards, when the same subject was one of the matters considered. I fancy Mr. Campbell will now see that I am about as advanced as
he is for free trade. I should like to have him with me for direct taxation.
I wish to extend direct taxation for imperial purposes ; also, I wish to apply
the same principle for Local Taxation, because this system would enlarge the
trade of the country immensely, cause a greater demand for the labour of
the working classes, which would give them more wages and purchasing
power for home necessaries and comforts, which, again, would increase our
foreign and home trades in the manufacturing districts. Besides which,
direct taxation takes very much less money out of the pockets of the consumers for imperial purposes than the other branch of our system of indirect
taxation. The ratepayers would be astounded could they understand the
difference that would be made to them by an extended system of direct
taxation under the income and property tax schedules as compared to our
present system.

I may say that I have never written one word against pulling down the
houses in narrow courts or narrow streets as such. That which I have
written is that a case has not yet been made out that court or front houses
generate the fevers, scarlatina, and diarrhœa. If drunkenness is the cause,
that should be attacked instead of the houses. Pull the houses down and
leave drunkenness alive, how much better shall we be after the expenditure
of nearly £300,000 ? True, taxation will be increased by the expenditure,
but will the death rate be decreased ? Certainly there would be one good
result from the expenditure—namely, that a number of the houses and
streets would have disappeared at the expense of poor tenants, as Mr. Campbell puts it, without any contribution towards the result out of nett profits
by personalty, which, in my opinion, is wrong in principle.

32, Castle-street. O. WILLIAMS.

APPENDIX.

(See Mr. O. Williams's Letters on pages 15 to 32.)

Table showing all the DEATHS from FEVER, SCARLATINA, and DIARRHŒA in the City of Liverpool during the TWO years, 1881 and 1882, according to the Reports of the Medical Officer of Health, in the following Streets:— In Front Houses, 635. In Back Houses, 329. Excess in Front Houses, 306.

STREETS AND ROADS.	Fever.		Scarlatina.		Diarrhœa.	
	Front House	Back House	Front House	Back House	Front House	Back House
Ascot	...	...	...	...	3	...
Addison	4	2	...	...	1	2
Aspinall	...	...	4	...	...	...
Aldersey	2	...	...	...	...	...
Arley	...	...	...	...	...	3
Ashfield	...	...	4	...	...	...
Athol	...	...	3	...	3	...
Arkwright	1	1	11	3	2	1
Arlington	2	...	5	...	...	...
Aughton	...	...	3	...	...	...
Anthony	...	...	...	...	3	...
Beacon	...	2	...	...	...	...
Beau	1	5	...	...	...	...
Bispham	2	...	...	...	2	4
Blandford	2	1	...	...	...	...
Blenheim	...	4	...	...	...	...
Bostock	2	...	3	...	2	1
Brownlow Hill	2	...	...	...	...	...
Beaufort	4	...	4	...	8	...
Beresford Street	...	4	...	...	...	...
Beresford Road	...	...	3	...	...	...
Boundary	1	1	3	2	...	...
Buckingham	2	...	...	...	3	...
Bulwer	2	...	...	...	...	...
Birchfield	...	...	5	...	...	...
Burlington	...	...	1	2	4	3
Beatrice	3	...	6	...	...	...
Ben Johnson	3	4	...	...	...	...
Blackstock	...	2	...	...	...	...
Blucher	1	1	...	...	...	...
Boaler	2	...	...	...	...	...
Carried Forward	36	27	55	7	31	14

c

STREETS AND ROADS.	Fever.		Scarlatina.		Diarrhœa.	
	Front House	Back House	Front House	Back House	Front House	Back House
Brought Forward......	36	27	55	7	31	14
Brindley	...	2	...	...	...	...
Black Bull Lane	...	...	3	...	...	...
Bosnia	...	...	3	...	...	...
Bunyan ...	...	...	3	...	...	...
Birkett	...	...	...	...	4	...
Brasenose Road...	...	...	...	...	5	...
Cooper	2	...	...	...	...	...
Cameron	...	...	3	...	...	...
Cockerell	...	...	3	...	...	...
Conway ...	...	...	3	...	...	...
Christian	...	...	...	5	3	1
Carlton ...	10	9	...	4	...	...
Cavendish	3	1	...	...	...	...
Cazneau...	4	...	...	...	...	3
Chadwick	1	3	...	...	...	...
Chapel Lane	1	2	...	...	...	...
Chatham	...	...	3	...	...	...
China ...	...	...	3	...	...	...
Charters	1	3	...	...	...	...
Cherry Lane	2	...	...	...	...	...
Chisenhale ...	2	...	...	...	2	5
Circus ...	4	...	...	...	2	1
Clement	2	...	...	...	...	...
Comus ...	...	3	...	...	...	...
Cuerdon	1	2	...	...	...	...
Chapman	1	2	...	...	...	...
Christopher ...	...	2	...	...	...	...
Combermere	1	2	...	...	...	...
Clive ...	...	...	...	...	1	2
Denbigh...	2	...	...	...	...	...
Darnley	2	...	...	...	...	...
Dalrymple	...	...	...	3	3	...
Darwen	2	...	...	...	3	...
Dryden ...	...	4	...	...	3	5
Duckinfield ...	2	2	...	...	1	2
Dalton ...	...	3	...	...	...	...
Eaton	1	4	...	...	...	...
Eccles ...	2	4	...	...	...	...
Elias ...	2	...	7	...	3	...
Ennerdale	...	...	...	...	2	1
Essex	3	...	...	...	3	...
Carried Forward....	87	75	86	19	66	34

STREETS AND ROADS.	Fever.		Scarlatina.		Diarrhœa.	
	Front House	Back House	Front House	Back House	Front House	Back House
Brought Forward....	87	75	86	19	66	34
Eden	..	..	3	..	..	..
Egerton	2	..	..	..	..	..
Eldon Street	..	..	..	..	..	3
Eldon Place	2	..	..	..	..	..
Everton Terrace	2	..	..	..	..	..
Everton Brow	..	..	3	..	..	..
Ford	1	4	..	..	..	..
Fletcher	2	..	..	..	..	..
Forth	..	..	..	..	3	..
Frederick	3	..	..	..	..	..
Fernie	1	2	..	..	..	..
Great Richmond	4	..	4	3	..	..
Gerard	7	..	..	..	..	..
Gordon	12	..	..	..	3	..
Gildart's Gardens	..	..	..	..	1	2
Great Howard	2	..	5	..	..	..
Grosvenor	2	..	..	..	..	..
Garibaldi	4	..	..	..	..	..
Glover	2	1	..	..	..	..
Grafton	3	..	6	1	3	2
Henry Edward	1	1	..	..	2	1
Hornby	..	4	1	2	4	6
Heriot	..	..	3	..	..	..
Harding	..	..	..	..	1	3
Hodson	..	2	..	..	..	..
Harold	..	..	..	..	4	..
Howe	4	..	..	..	3	..
Hopwood	2	..	..	..	..	..
High Park	..	..	3	..	..	..
Hyslop	..	..	..	3	..	..
Haliburton	3	..	..	..	..	..
Henderson	1	2	2	1	..	..
Hill	2	..	..	..	..	..
Hygeia	1	2	..	..	..	..
Islington	..	..	4	..	..	..
Jenkinson	1	6	..	..	..	..
Jackson	..	..	4	..	..	..
Kirkdale Road	2	..	..	..	..	..
Kew	..	..	..	..	1	2
Llanrwst	..	2	..	..	..	..
Lamb	2	..	..	..	..	..
Carried Forward.....	155	101	124	29	91	53

STREETS AND ROADS.	Fever.		Scarlatina.		Diarrhœa.	
	Front House	Back House	Front House	Back House	Front House	Back House
Brought Forward....	155	101	124	29	91	53
Limekiln Lane	..	..	..	..	3	1
Leander ..	2	..	..	..	..	..
Lancaster	3	..	..	..	..	..
Low Hill	..	..	..	..	..	3
Lowndes	4	..	..	..	..	..
Lithotimer	..	..	3	..	..	..
Lower Milk ..	2	..	..	..	..	..
Low Wood	..	..	1	2	..	..
Leyden	..	..	..	..	4	..
Mann	5	8	1	5	2	1
Mill ..	4	..	..	..	..	..
Minto	3	..	..	..	..	..
Maguire	1	3	..	..	..	..
Milton	2	7	..	..	..	..
Menai	..	..	2	2	..	..
Milford ..	..	..	3	..	..	.
Mill Road	..	..	3	..	..	..
Mitylene ..	..	..	3	..	..	..
Marlborough	3	..	..	..	..	..
Marybone	2	..	..	..	..	..
Mersey	..	2	..	..	..	..
Midghall Lane ..	2	..	..	..	..	..
Midghall	..	2	2	2	..	..
Mile End	1	1	..	..	..	..
Mount View, Rathbone Street	1	2	..	..	..	..
Major	2	..	..	..	..	..
Mark	2	..	..	..	..	..
Marwood	2	..	..	..	..	..
Naylor	..	5	..	.	..	3
Northumberland	2	..	1	3	..	..
Newsham ..	..	..	1	2	..	..
Nash	..	2	..	..	..	..
Netherfield Road North ..	3	..	..	..	..	..
Oriel	3	8	..	..	..	..
Opie ..	..	..	3	..	..	..
Paul	2	4	..	..	2	1
Portland Street	3	1	3	..	..	..
Portland Place ..	4	..	..	..	..	..
Primrose Hill	3	1	..	..	..	..
Paulton ..	2	..	..	..	..	..
Peach	3	..	..	..	..	..
Carried Forward....	221	147	150	45	102	62

STREETS AND ROADS.	Fever.		Scarlatina.		Diarrhœa.	
	Front House	Back House	Front House	Back House	Front House	Back House
Brought Forward....	221	147	150	45	102	62
Pickop	1	1	..	..	..	..
Pitt ..	4	..	..	..	..	..
Pownall Square	1	2	..	..	..	..
Pansy	..	..	..	..	3	..
Park Road	..	..	..	..	3	..
Pecksniff	..	..	..	..	3	..
Prescot ..	2	..	..	..	..	..
Prince Edwin	..	3	..	..	2	1
Prince William ..	..	2	..	..	..	..
Rosalind	..	..	..	..	4	.
Richmond Row ..	..	..	..	..	4	3
Rachel	..	..	..	4	..	..
Robsart ..	2	..	3	4	4	1
Rose Vale ..	..	..	1	2	..	..
Raymond	..	..	..	..	5	1
Robertson ..	..	..	..	..	3	..
Redmond Place..	3	3	..	..	..	..
Regent	2	2	..	..	..	..
Rice	..	2	..	..	..	..
Rose Place ..	1	1	..	..	1	2
Rankin ..	3	..	..	..	..	..
Rishton	2	..	..	..	..	..
Roscoe Street	..	..	..	3	..	..
Roscoe Lane..	..	..	..	..	1	2
Reading ..	..	..	..	..	3	..
Roscommon ..	..	..	..	..	2	1
Spring Place, Springfield Street	2	..	..	..	..	..
Smith	2	..	..	..	..	..
Stitt	..	..	6	..	..	..
Star ..	2	..	..	..	..	..
Saltney ..	1	1	..	..	1	5
Scotland Road	2	..	..	..	3	1
Steel	..	..	4	..	6	..
Sherwood ..	..	..	3	..	..	..
St. Andrew	3	..	..	..	..	..
Salisbury ..	2	..	..	..	..	..
Shaw ..	2	..	..	..	..	..
Sawney Pope	6	1	..	..	..	..
Silvester ..	3	..	..	..	..	..
Stancliffe ..	2	..	..	..	..	..
Stanhope	1	2	..	..	..	..
Carried Forward....	270	167	167	58	150	79

STREETS AND ROADS.	Fever.		Scarlatina.		Diarrhœa.	
	Front House	Back House	Front House	Back House	Front House	Back House
Brought Forward....	270	167	167	58	150	79
Slade	1	1	..	..	..	..
Sparling ..	5	..	..	..	..	..
Summer Gardens ..	2	..	..	..	..	..
Tatlock ..	1	1	..	..	2	2
Thurlow	2	1	..	..	1	2
Trueman	2	..	..	..	..	..
Upper Frederick ..	5	..	..	..	2	1
Upper Milk	..	2	..	..	..	..
Vauxhall Road	2	3	..	..	3	1
Webster ..	..	..	3	..	..	..
Woodstock ..	1	1	1	3	..	..
Warwick	2	1	..	..	..	..
Wolfe	4	1	..	..	..	..
Worthington	1	1	..	..	..	..
Wellington ..	2	..	..	..	..	..
Westmoreland ..	3	..	..	..	..	..
Whitley	..	4	..	..	..	..
Zante ..	..	..	3	..	..	..
Total...	303	183	174	61	158	85

Deaths from Fever alone in the years 1881 and
1882 in Front and Back Houses:—

Tradesmen 187.

Labourers 173.

MR. JOHN MURPHY'S LETTER ON INSANITARY DWELLINGS.

A Means to Improve them.

To the Editors of the Liverpool Mercury.

GENTLEMEN,

Since the Marquis of Salisbury revived the question of improved dwellings for the working classes, the agitation of the subject has spread through the country with almost reckless impetuosity. The subject, too, has been so undeliberately adopted by local governing bodies as to lead them into the hasty concoction of schemes for the erection of workmen's dwellings, which would not only seriously injure the rights of property, but increase the already too burdensome amount of local taxation to an almost ruinous extent. Fancy the Liverpool City Council, after their management of the Nash Grove scheme, being trusted by the ratepayers with the spending of £200,000 for the problematical advantage of becoming cottage owners! Let the ratepayers look to it. "'Tis a good round sum." Yet that may be but a comparatively small beginning of the expenditure which they may incur on the doubtful project. For their newly inflamed zeal for "bricks and mortar" may hurry them on in a reckless course of extravagance. So let the ratepayers be prepared to check it.

Though several remedies have been proposed in connection with insanitary dwellings, few of the advocates for improving them seem to have sufficiently considered the cause of the unhealthy and wretched condition in which so many of the working classes are domiciled. Hence, some parties lavishly expend their vituperation on the owners of the property, as if landlords are to blame for the improvidence of tenants, and for all the dirt, dilapidation, wretchedness, and misery in so great a number of the working people's homes. Hence, too, the landlords are said to be the greatest delinquents, who should suffer severe punishment and submit to the exaction of heavy penalties, even to the confiscation of their properties, which in their unjust censoriousness, the advocates of improved dwellings would inflict. One of our local Solons, for instance, exercising his conscience as if he had forgotten to renew his acquaintance with justice, stated his approval of a plan elsewhere in operation 'tis said where "they prosecuted the owners of bad property first and compensated them afterwards." Thus, on the "deliver or die" principle, an unfortunate owner of "bad property" would be harassed and wearied by the prosecutions, amounting to persecutions, of a local governing body that could be so unjust until he would be compelled to part with his property on terms that might, in a pecuniary sense, be utterly ruinous to him. Such an outrageous doctrine, based upon such an unfair principle, must surely recoil upon any individual who preaches it, and upon any local authority that would put its precepts into practice, and so, by such teaching and example, be highly injurious to the true interests of the entire community. For such unprincipled conduct in a local governing body would have a tendency to militate against the rights of all classes of property—real and personal—and render the ownership of it less secure ; so that the evil consequences of so dealing with " bad property" would not altogether fall upon landlords.

But are the owners of the property to blame for the wretched state in which so many dwellings of the working classes are ? Surely not. The owners are not only not deserving of censure, but they are rather to be commiserated, for in most instances the property is both an incessant plague to them and a serious pecuniary loss. They are, besides, in some degree, benefactors of the working classes, because if it had not been for the builders and owners of cottage property the great mass of the labouring people who flocked here from all parts of the country and from other nations could not have been housed. For it was the builders and owners of such property who anticipated the necessity for housing an increasing population, and accordingly provided suitable dwellings to meet the domiciliary requirements of the continuously-augmenting numbers of the working people. But they could not by anticipation provide against the serious dilapidation and consequent depreciation of their properties through the dirty, drunken, pugnacious, and debased habits of consequently degraded and wretched tenants.

Let the following facts serve to show the class of tenants with which a landlord has occasionally to deal :—There is a good broad, well flagged court with an entrance to it of about 15ft. wide, in which there are six houses (three on each side), containing four apartments in each, which were let at a rent of 3s. per week for each house. The rent was previously higher, but the neighbourhood had "gone down." The rent was further reduced to 2s. 6d. per week, and let to tenants who were selected with "caution and care." But even that low rent was not properly paid, because the tenants soon showed that they favoured the publican more than the landlord. Some of them got drunk and quarrelled ; others, through their own indiscretion, were drawn into the fight ; for a word of praise or blame in a row soon brings the eyes of an indiscreet meddler in contact with the fist of a pugnacious partisan of one of the combatants. Then, after personal hostilities commenced, they, with pokers and other implements of brawling warfare, "cried havoc, and let slip the dogs of war" at each others houses, until the smashed windows, broken glass strewn about the court, shattered window shutters and doors showed how great and deplorable had been the destruction of the property. The houses thus, for a time, were rendered uninhabitable and the reckless tenants left them, to manufacture "insanitary property" elsewhere. The landlord thus got rid of bad tenants which, but for the "law's delay," he would have done before. The houses were afterwards put in "good order and condition," and re-let. But the new tenants had been there only a short time when two of them quarrelled, and one of them had in consequence to leave. Other instances could be adduced to show that such tenants are undeniably the cause of much that is called "insanitary property," as all persons know who have any practical acquaintance with the manners and customs of that almost irreclaimable class of the community. It is remarkable that some of the working people cannot " enjoy themselves," as they call it when they are " on the beer," without exercising their combative and destructive propensities ; and when spoken to about their vicious habits, they console themselves and partly justify their conduct by saying, "Ay, well, its a poor heart that never rejoices."

Since, however, the recent agitation for improved workmen's dwellings commenced, it is at length becoming more generally admitted that, what is in numerous instances, the insanitary condition of property arises from the debased habits of a certain class of tenants, and not, as it was at first said, by persons who had little or no experience of such tenants, through the "greed of landlords." Yet landlords have not the "greed" that prevents their keeping their houses in needful repair for deserving tenants rather than lose them, if from no other motive ; for landlords, like tradesmen, can appreciate a "good customer." But surely a landlord has no encouragement to continually spend considerable sums of money for tenants whose lives are a self-imposed misery, who keep their homes in a wretchedly filthy state destroy the landlord's property, and get drunk with the money that should pay the rent. Those philanthropic and wealthy individuals who, with false sympathy for such tenants, rail at the landlords and think that owners should incur a ceaseless expenditure for such undesirable tenants, and would so spend their money if they had the property, can doubtless readily place themselves in the position of landlords of such a class of tenants, and so find many opportunities for the exercise of their forbearance, generosity, and kindness, and thus learn to sacrifice self-interest for the advantage of the worthless. That, doubtless, many owners of the property would consider, is a "consummation devoutly to be wished." Such individuals, on their becoming landlords, would no doubt gladly undergo the many trials of patience and forbearance in their weary if not hopeless efforts to elevate the tenants and improve their dwellings ; though, as Lord Salisbury says, their "influence will hardly be felt until a more educated generation takes the place of that which now exists." Let, then, those individuals who are blaming the landlords, and who think that they can do better with the property than its present owners are doing, seek to invest their money in it, and "take heart for the work," keeping in view that "the untrained mind of debased humanity luxuriates on vicious habits, and leads man to grovel in his own degradation, decorate his dwelling as you may."

It being admitted, then, that bad tenants cause bad property, it only makes matters worse to blame the landlords for what the tenants should be censured. Because it induces lazy, dirty, and improvident tenants to consider themselves blameless in producing the wretched and filthy condition of their dwellings, and so prevents their doing anything to better their condition and improve the state of their houses. Many of such tenants even now believe that however they may dirty and destroy their houses the sanitary inspector will compel the landlord to clean and repair them. For, as some of them say when the rent is asked from them, and they are determined not to pay it even when they have it, "Al tell the Boord o' Health o' ya, an he'll soon make ya' do it." The action of the sanitary inspectors in sending so many "notices" to the owners, as if the inspectors vied with each other in their efforts to issue the greatest number, have no doubt caused the tenants to believe that the landlords are responsible for the cleanliness of their houses. Yet it may, after all, seem strange that a sanitary inspector can compel a landlord to whiten the ceilings and paper the walls of a house, though he cannot make a tenant wash a floor—even that on which his dirty straw bed is placed. Truly have Drs. Parkes and Sanderson said—" Whatever takes from the tenants the responsibility of cleanliness in their houses is wrong." Certainly every official discouragement should be given to dirty tenants.

As to the means of improving the condition of labourers' dwellings. It is absolutely necessary that landlords should have speedier means of getting rid of an incorrigible tenant, and greater facilities for obtaining possession of their occupied property, than the law now gives them. For under the present law weeks may elapse before a landlord can legally eject such a tenant, so that a refractory tenant may defy his landlord to interfere with him, however filthy such tenant may keep his house, and however he may have dilapidated its interior. Without the tenant's permission the landlord has no legal right to cross the threshold of his tenant's dwelling, because "an Englishman's house is his castle, and the King dares not enter it." Yet there are those who sympathise with the tenant and rail at the landlord for the insanitary condition of the house which the tenant has caused. But the landlord, though being thus kept out of possession of his property, has not yet sustained his greatest hardship; for the defiant tenant may, through his filthy habits have brought an infectious disease into his dirty dwelling. Then the active sanitary inspector, eager for business, sends the unfortunate landlord an imperative notice to clean down the house, which of course is done. The tenant then, seeing in his house the result of the inspector's authority over the landlord, stands in a defiant attitude, and with an air of independence tells his landlord to do his "best to turn him out." The house will not, of course, be long before it is again in an "insanitary" state. Such, however, is an instance of the influence which the action of sanitary inspectors, even in the exercise of their lawful occupation, has over ignorant minds, which are misled by the idea that sanitary inspectors are only to make landlords clean houses for perverse and dirty tenants. But with a law giving landlords full power to "effect a speedy clearance" of tenants whose habits allow filth to accumulate in their houses and to generate an infectious disease, a tenant would know that he must either keep his house clean or get notice to quit and be ejected. Then, with the landlord's refusal to let a house to a tenant who cannot bring a "good character from his last place," the difficulty which bad tenants would have in getting a house, and the necessity of overcoming it by better conduct, would soon produce an amendment in their habits and an improvement in their dwellings. The law should also make it a misdemeanour for any person to take possession of a house which has not been let to him by either the landlord or his agent. Nor should a sub-tenant be allowed to remain in the house against the will of the landlord after the principal tenant has "run away," or who has otherwise had to quit, but should be immediately compelled to leave.

Landlords would thus obtain a much-needed control over their property for its more efficient management, not only for their own interest, but for the advantage of the tenants and an improvement in the sanitary condition of their dwellings. Because with improved habits in the tenants and cleaner houses there would be fewer cases of zymotic disease and a lower death-rate, so that the result would be a benefit to the entire community. For, as Dr. Taylor, the medical officer of health, states in his last annual report, "There is a large and growing class amongst us who almost appear to be beyond the pale of enlightenment; while disease, fostered by their habits, is apt to break through the boundaries of unhealthy districts and spread its lethal shadow far and wide."

Let sanitary and social reformers, then, who desire to improve the dwellings of the working classes, direct their praiseworthy efforts to eradicate the improvident and debasing habits which cause the wretchedness, misery, and disease in so many of the labouring people's homes. Then, with better habits in tenants, there will be an improvement in the sanitary state of their dwellings, and with superior domestic arrangements there will be healthier and happier households.

JOHN MURPHY.

South John Street, Liverpool, Dec. 18, 1883.

SQUALID LIVERPOOL.

Your Council have read with very great interest the small pamphlet which is a collection of short letters which appeared in the *Daily Post* during the last few weeks under the above title. That which has made it the more interesting is that the picture drawn of Squalid Liverpool is, as nearly as may be, true to nature and life. In the description there is nothing coarse or repulsive to the reader. No untrue or unfair motives are attributed. Indeed it is surprising that this word-painter should not often have been tempted in some districts to have made some of the shades darker than they appear, and made others much brighter when the subject for it came across his path. On the whole the picture is admirably drawn; though, possibly, if the writer had taken up the brush in some districts some of the shading would not have been so dark. But this is to be expected; it is said that there are not even two blades of grass exactly alike, nor two shells on the sea shore. Likely there are not two minds exactly alike. This being so, each individual is a speciality, within a circle, to himself—and no two persons can therefore see the same picture exactly alike. Both may differ and the picture may still be true. Here and there are beautiful and tender touches, when the poor lone widow and the helpless little ones are found in such terrible poverty and degradation, linked to poor fallen humanity. No wonder that such words as those used by such a tender sympathy should have had seed and roots in them, and that the fruit should already have appeared above ground : What is the first fruit ? The reader is asked to read the following :—

The names are thus given in your Annual Report for two reasons, namely, for ready reference and that the reader may know and see the drawing power and influence of the truth when allowed to appear in its simplicity. It is a pity that the names of the gentlemen who made the survey of Squalid Liverpool are unknown, as the whole citizens are under great obligations to them :—

The Housing of the Poor in Liverpool.

At the Offices of the Liverpool Council of Education, a meeting was held yesterday of gentlemen favourable to the appointment of a local committee of inquiry into the subject of the insanitary dwellings of this city, and the general question of the housing of the poor.— Mr. S. G. Rathbone presided.—After a preliminary statement by Mr. Christopher Bushell as to the objects of the new committee, the following gentlemen who had previously signified their willingness to act, were formally appointed members of the committee of inquiry :—Mr. T. D. Hornby, chairman of the Dock Board ; Mr. S. G. Rathbone, chairman of the School Board ; Mr. S. Smith, M.P., Smith, Edwards & Co.,; Sir W. B. Forwood, Leech, Harrison & Co.; Mr. T. F. A Agnew, Agnew, Jones & Co.; Mr. Clarke Aspinall, city coroner; Mr. Thomas Baring, Baring Brothers & Co.; Mr. Alfred Bright, Bateson & Co.; Mr. Ralph Brocklebank, J.P., T. and J. Brocklebank; Mr. Thomas Brocklebank, J.P., T. and J. Brocklebank; Mr. H. Stewart Brown, Brown, Shipley & Co.; Mr. Edward Brown, J.P.; Mr. Christopher Bushell, J.P., chairman of the Liverpool Council of Education ; Mr. E. W. Cropper, gentleman ; Mr. William Crosfield, J.P., Messrs. Crosfield, Barrow & Co.; Mr. Arthur Earle, J.F.

Earles and King; Mr. Duncan Graham, Graham, Rowe & Co.; Mr. H. B. Gilmour, J.P., vice-chairman of School Board; Mr. Malcolm Guthrie, G. H. Lee & Co.; Mr. Robert Gladstone, J.P., Ogilvy, Gilanders & Co.; Mr. G. H. Horsfall, J.P., C. Horsfall & Sons; Mr. James Harrison, Thomas and James Harrison; Mr. T. H. Ismay, J.P., Ismay, Imrie & Co.; Mr. Henry Jump, J.P., Henry Jump & Sons; Mr. Edward Lawrence, J.P., E. Lawrence & Co.; Mr. Gilbert W. Moss, the North-Western Bank; Mr. S. Sandbach Parker. Sandbach, Tinne and Co.; Mr. T. S. Raffles, J.P., stipendiary magistrate; Mr. Joshua Sing, Powell and Sing; Mr. Alfred Turner, J.P.; Mr. A. T. H. Waters, M.D.; Mr. John Yates, sen., Yates, Son and Stananought. Of these gentlemen, the following were appointed the Executive Committee :— Mr. S. G. Rathbone, Sir W. B. Forwood, Mr. Alfred Bright, Mr. Edward Browne, Mr. Willam Crosfield, Mr. Malcolm Guthrie, Mr. Sandbach Parker, Mr. Joshua Sing, Mr. Alfred Turner, and Dr. Waters. Mr. Bushell was elected chairman of the General Committee, and Mr. E. W. Cropper was elected the honorary secretary. The next meeting of the committee was not fixed.

Your Council believe that the labour's of such a Committee of wealth and position must have a tendency to improve the condition of the lowest stratum of society as well as their dwellings. Improve the individual and you have already improved his cottage. "These people are what the conditions of their environment have made them," says the writer of the pamphlet; but another view of this question is—"put a low drunken fellow into a palace and he will soon turn it into a stye of filth, but put a frugal, honest, industrious and sober man into a stye and he will soon turn it into a palace."

The writer of the pamphlet has gathered together information and placed it before the public such as has been known to many of your Council; and to other owners of property for upwards of forty years. In a very short time this new Insanitary Committee will be suprised to find what difficulties surround owners of the smallest class of property, and how their houses are wrecked by tenants in their squabbles and fights.

What is to be done?

Should this Council wish to produce immediate good, it would be well for them to farm a few thousand of the worst habitations from the House Agents. A Committee having a large property might have caretakers and workmen constantly on the spot—to let, repair, and to see that the houses were kept clean by the inmates. Such a Committee—many being Justices of the Peace,—would have a deterring power on the tenants. At the Sylvester street houses are caretakers, who are constantly on the spot. An agent or an owner of a few houses could not so continuously exercise such an oversight. In this way the Committee would soon come to know the real causes of fever, scarlatina, diarrhœa, and other zymotic diseases—whether by houses or drunkenness.

Is Drunkenness the Cause?

Your Council in the most respectful manner ask the new Insanitary Committee to consider the following extracts from the exhaustive and able Report issued by the House of Lords on Intemperance, on the 29th of March, 1879. The Birmingham Town Council traced the principal cause of the Insanitary Condition of the people to Intemperance, and your Council believe that it has very much to do with the question :—

Mr. Chamberlain's Evidence.

" The Town Council of Birmingham has shown its desire to adopt the plan by a majority of 46 to 10, while it has received the unanimous approval of the Board of Guardians. These number together about 120 gentlemen, representing directly a population of nearly 400,000 persons."

" The control of the local authority (should be had) over the issue of licenses."

" A great diminution in the number of public-houses and an improvement in their convenience, healthiness, and management would result."

" As the net results of the change, a diminution in intemperance, a reduction in crime and disorder, and a considerable balance of profit to be devoted to the relief of local rates."

" It would seem somewhat hard when such communities are willing, at their own cost and hazard, to grapple with the difficulty and undertake their own purification, that the legislature should refuse to create for them the necessary machinery, or to entrust them with the requisite powers."

" If it succeeds, great public good will have been done ; if it fails the loss will affect only the community which has committed itself to the experiment."

" The Committee, therefore, are of opinion that legislative facilities should be afforded for the adoption of those schemes, or some modification of them."

Summary of Recommendations.

" That legislative facilities should be afforded for the local adoption of the Gothenburg and of Mr. Chamberlain's schemes, or of some modification of them."

" That legal sanction should be obtained for the trial of either the Gothenburg or of Mr. Chamberlain's scheme, on the application to that effect from local authorities."

Your Council agree with the Commissioners of Squalid Liverpool that the streets are in a filthy condition ; go when you will where the poorest are located the stench is almost intolerable, by reason of the deposits from chamber utensils, ashes and all kinds of other filth. Most certainly the sights in very many instances are even worse than in the days of the ashpits ; whole streets and courts now are used

D

for such deposits. Arrangements should at once be made for proper binns for ashes and other refuse. And the sights in the Trough Closets are revolting; how can it be otherwise? Persons entering them in the dark can never be safe from filth. The City Council have rendered a good service to the poor in the courts by having caused them to be lighted. And it is hoped they will take another step forward by causing a jet of light to be introduced into each Trough Closet. It is easy to imagine what a boon this would be to the female sex in particular; as it would put an end to the sickening sights described by the Commission.

The Commission seem to be under the impression that when property is purchased by the Corporation that it is made on the gross rental; this is not so. Always on net rentals. Deductions are always made for empties, taxes, repairs, &c.; and the purchase is made on the net rentals,which are often very low indeed after all the deductions are made.

Your Council are certain that the Commission were shocked to see how property is wrecked by the drunkards and children. And it is felt that the police might do very much more service than they do if they apprehended the parties doing the damage. A few days' imprisonment of some of the destructive people would soon lessen the evils complained of. Property contributes very largely to the support of the police, and property is entitled to more consideration by the Watch Committee.

A graphic description is given of the neighbourhood of All Saints' Lane, by reason of the overcrowding, as there are disturbances there almost nightly, "Often the police dare not show their faces up it," say the Commission. A lesson should be taken from this fact, not to crowd too many together, as is proposed by the decker system of building. No doubt whatever—the proper system is to spread the working classes over as large an area as possible.

On the following page a table is prepared giving the names of about all the streets named by the Commissioners, and showing the deaths from fever, scarlatina, and diarrhœa during the two years, 1881 and 1882. It will be seen that there were not any deaths from the above diseases in several of the worst streets named, which surprises your Council very much after the descriptions given of them.

It will be seen that most deaths were in front houses; many of them being in wide streets.

The greatest death-rate was in Carleton street in 1882; in the previous year there was not a death in it from any of the above diseases, proving that the houses did not cause those diseases. If in one year of course the result would be pretty uniform each year. Often clean sober tenants leave, and low drunken ones take their places, which explains the different results.

Your Council recommend Squalid Liverpool to be read by all, with the following table in hand.

Table showing deaths from Fever, Scarlatina and Diarrhœa during the years 1881 and 1882 according to the Reports of the Medical Officer of Health, in the Streets visited by the *Daily Post* Commission in November, 1883, called "Squalid Liverpool."

STREETS AND ROADS.	Fever.		Scarlatina.		Diarrhœa.	
	Front House	Back House	Front House	Back House	Front House	Back House
All Saints' Lane	...	...	...	...	...	...
Bent and Back Milton ...	...	..	...	...	...	...
Ben Johnson ..	3	4	...	...	...	...
Britton	..	...	...	...	...	...
Byrom	...	...	...	...	...	...
Banastre...	...	...	...	...	...	...
Carlton	10	9	...	4	...	...
Cazneau	4	..	...	...	...	3
Comus	...	3	...	...	...	...
Cavendish	3	1	...	...	...	...
Dale ...	...	...	...	...	...	...
Fontenoy	...	...	...	...	...	...
Freemason's ...	...	...	...	...	...	...
Gay and Edgar ...	...	...	...	...	...	...
Gildart's Gardens	...	...	...	...	1	2
Great Howard ...	2	..	5	...	...	...
Great Crosshall	...	...	...	...	...	...
Graham Place ...	...	...	...	...	...	...
Harrison	...	...	...	...	...	...
Henry Edward	1	1	...	...	2	1
Henderson ...	1	2	2	1	...	...
Hodson	...	2	...	...	...	...
Lace ...	...	...	...	...	...	...
Mann	5.	8	1	5	2	1
Marybone	2	...	...	...	...	...
Northumberland	2	...	1	3	...	...
North...	...	...	...	...	...	...
Richmond	...	...	...	...	4	3
Rose Place ...	1	1	..	...	1	2
Scotland	2	...	...	...	3	1
Sawney Pope	6	1	...	...	...	...
Sherwood	...	..	3	...	...	...
Vauxhall	2	3	..	...	3	1
Woolfe ...	4	1	...	...	...	...
Warwick	2	1	...	...	...	...
Whitley	...	4	...	...	...	..
Total......	50	41	12	13	16	14

Your Council are afraid that the terrible descriptions given of some of the streets and properties, named in the pamphlet known as Squalid Liverpool, may cause alarm to mortgagees and loss to the Owners of Property; it will not be out of place, therefore, to make a few remarks on some of the streets therein named, about 38 streets are named in the pamphlet, and therefore in the above table. Nothwithstanding the descriptions and awful pictures drawn, it seems curious and strange that out of the 38 streets named it appears, from the Reports of the Medical Officer of Health, for the years 1881 and 1882, there was not a single death from fever, scarlatina, or diarrhœa in 16 of them. And in several of the other streets, there were only a very few deaths in the two years as is seen on preceding page. And this, too, in the very lowest streets of the town, besides which, most deaths were in fine wide roads.

In the pamphlet FONTENOY-STREET is described as being "as dirty, as tumble-down, and as unhealthy as any portion of Squalid Liverpool." But no deaths from the above diseases.

LACE-STREET is described "as another fever-stricken locality." No deaths.

GRAHAM-PLACE "is one of the queerest bits of Squalid Liverpool," according to the views of the writer. But no deaths.

The death-bed scene in NORTH-STREET, so graphically described, must really be read by the reader—the description is really very sad. This street seems to be the point of the whole pamphlet. The extract cannot be given for want of room, still no death in it is recorded for the 2 years above-named of fever, scarlatina, or diarrhœa.

Banastre-street is described as "a spectacle to be witnessed which cannot be seen anywhere else in Liverpool." No deaths.

Freemason's-row comes in for a graphic description and picture which occupies nearly two pages; still no deaths.

Harrison-street and Back Milton-street are down as "horrible slums," but no deaths. Bent-street and Edgar-street have a speciality of their own; but no deaths.

Britton-street is said to have been a hot bed of fever for the last four years, and "in one house a man and his wife both died." No deaths are reported in the Medical Officer of Health's Reports for 1881 and 1882, in this street.

In the opinion of your Council it is made pretty plain by the contents of the above tables that houses are not the cause of the high death rate from fever, scarlatina, and diarrhœa in Liverpool. If they are, of course a large crop of those diseases would have been found in many of the streets above named in which there was not a single case during the years 1881 and 1882. Drunkenness, undoubtedly is the cause. The Commissioners visited the streets in old Liverpool. If they will take a ramble through new streets and new houses near the new Bootle docks and in Seaforth and Waterloo, plenty of subjects will be met with for the work of the pen, almost, if not quite as revolting as those in Liverpool, as the product of drunkenness and immorality is not confined to old houses and narrow or old streets.

www.ingramcontent.com/pod-product-compliance
Lightning Source LLC
Chambersburg PA
CBHW021641270326
41931CB00008B/1117